After Life

Ways We Think About Death

MERRIE-ELLEN WILCOX

ORCA BOOK PUBLISHERS

Library and Archives Canada Cataloguing in Publication

Wilcox, Merrie-Ellen, author
After life : ways we think about death / Merrie-Ellen Wilcox.

Includes bibliographical references and index.

Issued in print and electronic formats.
ISBN 978-1-4598-1388-5 (hardcover).—ISBN 978-1-4598-1390-8 (PDF).—
ISBN 978-1-4598-1391-5 (EPUB)

1. Death—Juvenile literature. 2. Funeral rites and
ceremonies—Juvenile literature. I. Title.

GT3150 W543 2018   j393   C2017-907913-1
C2017-907914-X

First published in the United States, 2018
Library of Congress Control Number: 2018933700

Summary: This nonfiction book for middle-grade readers examines the history, beliefs and customs surrounding death in cultures around the world.

Orca Book Publishers is dedicated to preserving the environment and has printed this book on Forest Stewardship Council® certified paper.

Orca Book Publishers gratefully acknowledges the support for its publishing programs provided by the following agencies: the Government of Canada through the Canada Book Fund and the Canada Council for the Arts, and the Province of British Columbia through the BC Arts Council and the Book Publishing Tax Credit.

Interior watercolor illustrations by MimiPrints

Edited by Sarah N. Harvey
Design by Teresa Bubela
Interior photos: p. 46 © Jan Reurink, https://www.flickr.com/photos/reurinkjan/;
p. 47 © Julia Maudlin, https://creativecommons.org/licenses/by/4.0/.
Front cover photos: kaleigh/iStock.com and Dennis van de Water/Shutterstock.com
Back cover photos: rightdx/iStock.com and jorisvo/Shutterstock.com
Front flap photo: Kzenon/Shutterstock.com
Back flap author photo: Tsenka Dianova

ORCA BOOK PUBLISHERS
orcabook.com

Printed and bound in Canada.

21 20 19 18 • 4 3 2 1

For my mother, Wendy, whose love and courage will always inspire me.
And in memory of Joy, whose love of life lives on.

Contents

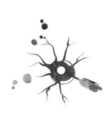
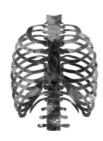

A NOTE FOR PARENTS, TEACHERS AND OTHER CARING ADULTS

As with many things in life, not talking about death can just make it bigger and scarier. By looking at death in terms of both the natural world and human culture, introducing readers to some modern terms and concepts, and speaking about the experience of grief and loss, I have tried to open the door, if only just a crack, to a healthy and thoughtful discussion about this great mystery.

Introduction

From the beginning of our history, humans have sung, danced, painted and written about death. But these days we don't talk much about death, especially around kids. Why is that? All human beings die, after all—and with almost eight billion of us on the planet, there's a lot of dying going on.

Death has always been mysterious. Just as babies can't look back and tell us anything about where they were before they were born, no one who dies can come back to tell us where they went and what it was like. So we've always tried to understand and explain not only what happens to us when we are no longer living, but also how we should live our lives to make sure that what happens after we die is good.

In the last century, though, the way we deal with death has changed. Especially in places where advances in medicine and public health have helped people live much longer, most people die in hospital now rather than at home. *Undertakers* at funeral homes, rather than our families, take care of our bodies when we die. Because we rarely see and experience it up close, death seems more mysterious than ever.

When I was growing up, death was around—my baby sister died days after she was born, my friend's father died suddenly, and my twelve-year-old classmate died when he was hit by a car. But I didn't attend a funeral or see a dead body until my grandmother died, when I was in my early twenties.

Much later I was with my sister-in-law when she died, surrounded by her family. Joy's death was tragic and terribly sad, but being with her and her extended family at that moment was one of the most important experiences in my life. Not long afterward, I became involved in my community's **hospice**, a place where people who are dying receive special care, so I got to think a lot about death and dying. That's how I came to write this book.

Why do we die? Why don't we live forever? What happens when we die? Even the earliest human beings, hundreds of thousands of years ago, grappled with these questions. This book looks at some of the answers modern science provides, as well as what a few of the world's cultures and religions, past and present, tell us about this greatest of mysteries. Each chapter includes a story or history from an ancient or Indigenous culture. Some of these might seem familiar to you, because there are so many different versions of the same story in different cultures. In the last chapter, we also look at **grief**, the process we go through after someone close to us has died.

Since death is something we don't talk about very much, some of the facts and ideas in *After Life* might surprise you. I hope the book will interest you and answer some of your questions. But if you find anything upsetting or worrying, please don't keep it to yourself. Talk to an adult you trust. May *After Life* be the beginning of many good conversations.

A boy visits a grave in a Muslim cemetery. ZURIJETA/SHUTTERSTOCK.COM

In a military cemetery, a family gathers to remember someone—a father, husband and son—who has died. WHL/GETTY IMAGES

CHAPTER ONE

We Are Stardust

Earth was formed around five billion years ago, when gases and dust from the explosions of giant stars came together. Today everything on and in our beautiful blue planet is made from that same stardust. Every rock and every living thing contains those first atoms, which have been recycled over and over and over since our planet was formed. And, yes, *every living thing* includes you and me.

The human body contains about seven octillion (that's seven followed by twenty-seven zeros!) atoms, almost all of them hydrogen, oxygen, carbon or nitrogen atoms. Since all of those atoms have been endlessly recycled since Earth's formation, it's quite possible that some of the atoms in your body were once in a dinosaur or a strange creature at the bottom of the sea, a giant sequoia tree or a tiny alpine flower near the top of a mountain.

Like all other living things, humans die. And when we die, those zillions of atoms we contain will be recycled once again and returned to the great pool of matter and energy from which all of life flows. We are simply part of a giant cycle of life and death.

The atoms in the stardust and gases that came together to form Earth are the same ones that we are made from. YUSUF YILMAZ/ SHUTTERSTOCK.COM

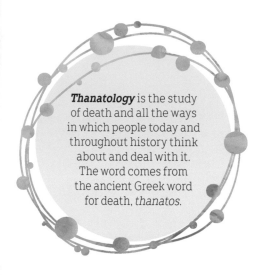

RISING FROM THE ASHES

In the myths of ancient Egypt and Greece, the phoenix is a symbol of immortality and resurrection. Only one of these birds could exist in the world at a time, and it could live for somewhere between 500 and almost 1,500 years. When it sensed that its life was nearing its end, the phoenix would build a nest and set it on fire. It would then be consumed by the flames, and a new phoenix would rise from the ashes.
ELLERSLIE/SHUTTERSTOCK.COM

THE AFTERLIFE

It's natural for us to fear death. Like most other living things on earth, even plants, we are "hardwired" to protect ourselves and fight for our lives. But human beings can also *think* about life and death, and create stories to explain them and **rituals** to mark them, as every human culture has done since human culture began. And in every culture, both in history and today, we can see evidence of our desire for an **afterlife**— some kind of continuation of ourselves after death.

Ideas about the afterlife are almost as varied as human beings are. But there are some patterns. For example, people in most cultures believe there is something other than our physical body, a spirit or **soul** that joins our body before we are born and leaves it when we die.

Some people believe that, like the atoms that make up the human body, the human spirit or soul is part of a giant cycle, coming back to life after death over and over again. This is called **reincarnation**. Others believe the soul doesn't come back but carries on forever in some other realm that can't be seen by the living.

In most versions of the afterlife, though, how people live their lives here on earth will determine what happens after they die.

RECYCLING SOULS

The idea of the human soul or spirit being recycled has been around for thousands of years. The belief that the soul of a person who dies will be reborn in another body is found in religions and cultures all over the world, again with many variations.

One of the best known of these is in Hinduism. Hindus believe that after a person's death the soul returns to a new body. Whether the new life is better or worse than the one before depends on how that person lived his or her life, an idea known as *karma*. A person who lives well and practices his or her religion in each life will eventually be released from the cycle of rebirth and achieve *nirvana*, becoming one with the infinite spirit. Buddhism shares with Hinduism some of the same beliefs about karma and nirvana.

Unlike Hindus and Buddhists, people in many West African cultures believe that life on earth is better than a permanent life of the spirit and that rebirth is a good thing. People are generally reborn into the same family. Sometimes one soul will die in an infant or young child and be born into the same family over and over again.

Some of the ancient Greek philosophers also believed in reincarnation. Plato taught that the soul is immortal (it lives forever) and is reborn many times, choosing its next life based on its experiences in past lives. But Aristotle, one of Plato's students, rejected his teacher's ideas of reincarnation and *immortality*. He believed the soul couldn't be separated from the body, so it couldn't live on after a person died.

LIFE IN ANOTHER REALM

Many cultures throughout human history have believed in a place where souls go after death—in some cases, to be judged.

For example, the ancient Egyptians believed that after death the soul went on a long, dangerous journey through the *underworld*, deep within the earth. People spent their whole

The Greek philosophers Plato (left) and his star student, Aristotle. RAPHAEL/WIKICOMMONS

NEAR-DEATH EXPERIENCES

Many people who come very close to dying describe experiences like leaving or floating above their bodies or moving through a dark tunnel toward a bright light. Or they see people they love who have died either telling them to come to them or telling them to go back.

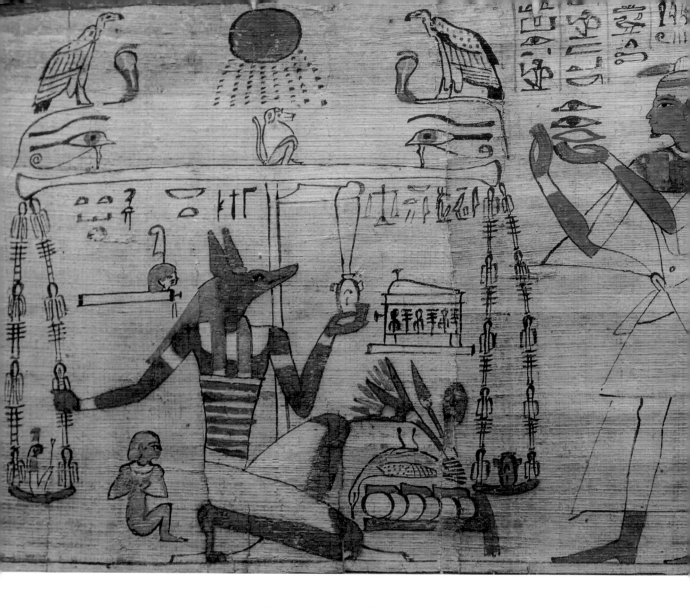

In this picture from an Egyptian *Book of the Dead*, the god Anubis weighs a heart on a scale. If the heart is as light as a feather, the soul of the dead person is considered virtuous and will go on to paradise. If the heart is heavier, it will be eaten by the goddess Ammit, and the soul will be lost forever.

lives preparing for this journey. The soul would encounter evil serpents, five-headed reptiles and other scary creatures. It also had to pass through seven gates, reciting a spell at each one. (The spells were included in the Egyptian **Book of the Dead**, a copy of which would be placed in the coffin so the soul could use it.) Finally, the soul had to convince forty-two divine judges that it had done no wrong. Then its heart would be weighed on a scale. If the soul's heart was innocent and good, it would be as light as a feather, and Osiris, god of the underworld, would welcome the soul to paradise. If the heart was heavier than a feather, the soul was devoured and gone forever.

In most forms of Islam, Judaism and Christianity there is also a kind of weighing of souls after death. People are judged on things like how good they have been in the practice of their faith. In some traditions, those who have been good are rewarded by going to heaven, where they will forever be with God. The others go to hell, forever separated from God. Some groups, especially among Christians, also believe that the dead will eventually be **resurrected**, or brought back to life.

In ancient Egypt, models of boats were often placed in tombs with the dead to help them in their journey to the afterlife. Pharaoh Khufu, who built the Great Pyramid, was buried with a boat that was more than 43 meters (140 feet) long. Many boats were about 6 meters (20 feet) long, and some were much smaller. But they all contained oars and people to row them, carved from wood. METROPOLITAN MUSEUM OF ART/ROGERS FUND AND EDWARD S. HARKNESS GIFT, 1920

ORPHEUS IN THE UNDERWORLD

In Greek mythology, Orpheus was the greatest of human musicians. He was given a lyre (a stringed instrument) by his father, Apollo, god of the arts, and trained by the Muses. The whole world loved his music.

Orpheus married the nymph Eurydice (pronounced "yu-**rid**-i-see"), but soon after, she was bitten by a snake and died. Overcome with grief, Orpheus went to the underworld to try to get her back. He used his music to charm **Hades**, the god of the underworld, and his wife, Persephone. They agreed to let Eurydice follow Orpheus back to the land of the living, as long as he didn't look back at her until they had both passed through the gates to the underworld.

They were almost at the gates when Orpheus glanced backward. Eurydice slipped back into the underworld forever. Orpheus begged to be allowed to try again, but to no avail. Orpheus finally returned to the world, without Eurydice, and from then on played only the saddest music. JEAN-BAPTISTE-CAMILLE COROT/WIKICOMMONS

RIVERS

Rivers play a role in the afterlife in many cultures. The souls of the dead often have to cross a river before they can enter the other realm for the afterlife. An old man usually takes them across, and sometimes a dog either guards the entrance to the other realm or is the souls' guide dog.

In Greek mythology, five rivers surrounded the underworld: Acheron (the river of woe), Cocytus (the river of lamentation), Phlegethon (the river of fire), Styx (the river of hatefulness) and Lethe (the river of forgetfulness). The souls of the dead drank from the River Lethe in order to forget their lives on earth.

When a person died, Hermes, the messenger of the gods, would deliver the soul to the entrance to the underworld. A ferry would be waiting to carry the soul across the River Acheron. Charon, the ferryman of the dead, would take the souls from bodies that had been properly buried with a silver coin under the tongue to pay the fare. He would throw any others out of his boat, and they would remain trapped between worlds forever.

On the other side of the river waited Cerberus, a three-headed dog also known as the Hound of Hades. Some stories say he also had a mane of snakes and the claws of a lion. Cerberus guarded the entrance to the underworld, a diamond gate, letting anyone enter—especially those who had been buried with honey cakes to bring to him—but keeping all from leaving. Once having entered the underworld, the souls then faced three judges, who sent those who had been good in life to a kind of heaven called the Elysian Fields. Those who had been bad were sentenced to eternal torment.

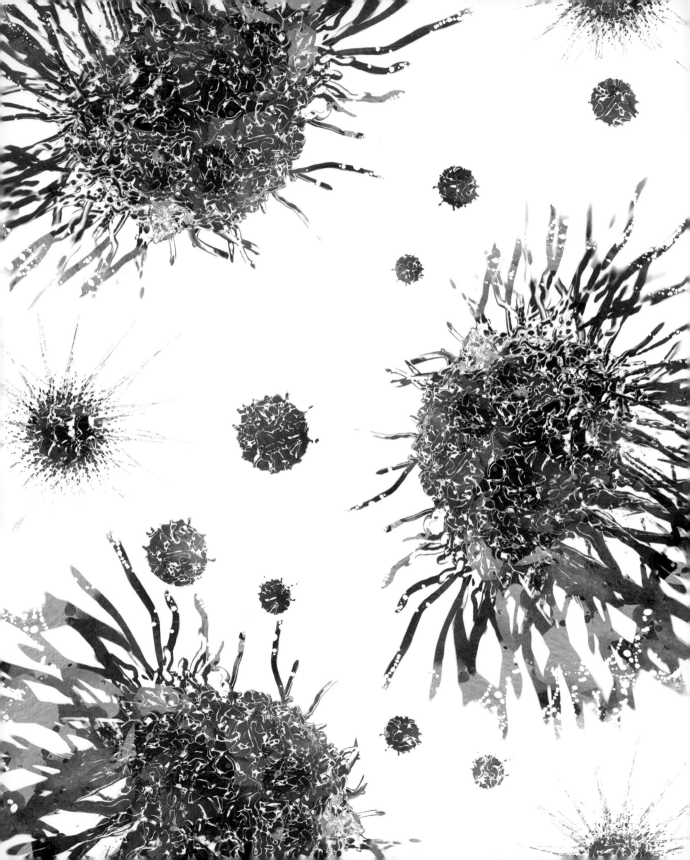

CHAPTER TWO

Every Living Thing

All living things (organisms), from the tiniest bacteria to the largest mammals, are born, grow up and die at their own pace. Humans are no different.

Every organism is made up of many different kinds of *cells*. Scientists estimate that a human body contains more than thirty-seven trillion (that's thirty-seven followed by twelve zeros) of them. Every day, almost ten billion of those cells die and are instantly replaced by new ones. Some cells, like certain ones in our intestines, last only a few days. Others, like some nerve cells (neurons), last for more than sixty years.

But this amazing ability of our cells to renew themselves weakens over time, and eventually things begin to break down. This is one part of what we call aging, the gradual buildup of different kinds of damage to the molecules and cells in our bodies. The systems of the body that keep us alive begin to work less and less well. Eventually, if we don't die from some other cause first, we just get worn out, and we die.

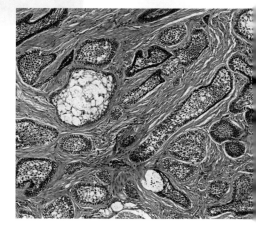

Human cells—dyed pink so they can be seen through a microscope. MRIMAN/ SHUTTERSTOCK.COM

IT'S ALL ABOUT OXYGEN

Not everyone dies of old age, of course. Many other things can cause death before old age does. They can be divided into four groups:

- illnesses (like cancer, heart disease, diabetes and genetic diseases)
- infections (like influenza, tuberculosis or malaria) caused by viruses, bacteria or protozoa
- poisons
- traumas (like accidents and violence)

Although these four causes of death work in different ways, they all stop the body from working by the same means: they block the supply of oxygen to the various organs in the body.

So whether death is caused by illness, infection, poison or trauma, it is always the result of a lack of oxygen.

HOW LONG DO WE LIVE?

Every kind of organism, whether plant or animal, has a *life span*—the length of time it can be expected to live. So how long do human beings live, anyway? Sounds like a simple question, right? It's not. Turns out there are different ways to think about it.

The human life span is the number of years that we could live under ideal conditions, in a healthy environment with our basic needs for food, water and shelter met. Some scientists believe that in *industrialized countries* (countries that have a complex economy based on lots of industry), we are getting close to our limit—somewhere between eighty-five

THE FOUR HORSEMEN OF THE APOCALYPSE

The Book of Revelation is the last book of the New Testament (part of the Christian Bible). It describes the Four Horsemen of the Apocalypse—four beings that appear on white, red, black and pale horses. Today the rider of the white horse is often known as Pestilence (infectious disease), War rides the red horse, and Famine rides the black horse, carrying scales for weighing out bread. Death rides on the pale horse, often shown as grayish green, the color of a *corpse*. Death is sometimes shown in paintings as the Grim Reaper, a skeleton carrying a scythe.
ZVONIMIR ATLETIC/SHUTTERSTOCK.COM

THE BLACK DEATH

Humans have always been afraid of contagious diseases—with good reason. The best-known example happened in the fourteenth century, when the **Black Death** swept through the Middle East and then through almost all of Europe. More than a third—maybe even half—of the people in Europe died over seven years, and the toll may have been higher in Asia and North Africa. It took the world's population three centuries to recover.

Medical historians believe the killer was a bacteria that infects rats. Fleas that fed on the dying rodents carried the bacteria to other victims, including humans, causing a disease known as *plague*. In the case of the Black Death, the rats lived in the holds of ships carrying goods from Asia for trading. The ships first brought the disease to Italy and Sicily, then to France, and from there it spread rapidly.

At the time no one understood how the disease spread or how to cure it. Doctors used the techniques of the day, such as bloodletting, as well as superstitious practices, such as burning herbs, to treat patients—or they refused to treat them at all. Many people believed that the disease was God's punishment for various sins.

Outbreaks of plague continued for centuries, though none were as devastating as the Black Death. Improvements in public health and medicine have all but eliminated plague, but today other diseases, such as influenza, ebola and HIV/AIDS, have taken its place as sources of fear around the world.

Top: During outbreaks of plague, doctors wore masks with birdlike beaks filled with dried flowers, herbs and spices, which they thought would protect them from the disease. Garlic was also believed to ward off plague, and you can see some hanging on this doctor's belt. MOREVECTOR/SHUTTERSTOCK.COM *Middle:* Fleas like this one spread the bacteria that cause plague. COSMIN MANCI/ADOBE STOCK *Bottom:* The Black Death is believed to have killed about 50 million people in Europe alone. ISTOCK.COM/ADAM STIELSTRA

and a hundred years. But others believe that things like better medicine and diet will allow humans to live much longer.

Life expectancy gives us a different kind of picture. It tells us how long people can expect to live, based on statistics. In 2015, life expectancy for the whole world was about seventy-one and a half years. This means that a baby born in 2015 can expect to live for just over seventy-one years.

But of course it's not quite that simple—it depends on whether that baby is a girl or a boy and on where she or he lives in the world. For example, life expectancy for women in most parts of the world is nearly five years longer than it is for men—almost seventy-four for women globally and just over sixty-nine for men. And life expectancy for a baby born in Africa is sixty years, compared with eighty-two years for one born in Canada and just over seventy-nine years in the United States.

THE BLUE ZONES

Researchers have discovered five places in the world where people live the longest. Known as the "blue zones," they are Sardinia, Italy; Ikaria, Greece; Okinawa, Japan; Nicoya, Costa Rica; and Loma Linda, California. No one is sure exactly why people live so long in the blue zones, but things they have in common include a good diet, hard work and a strong family and social life.

MAP OF THE BLUE ZONES

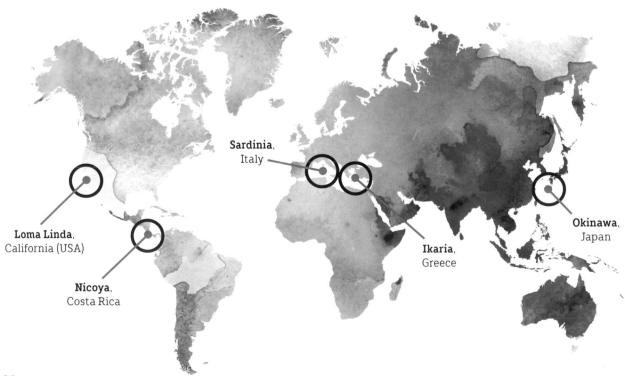

Sardinia, Italy

Loma Linda, California (USA)

Nicoya, Costa Rica

Ikaria, Greece

Okinawa, Japan

Of course, this doesn't mean that every baby born in 2015 is going to live for that many years. Life expectancy is based on averages, which means that some people will live longer and others will have a shorter life.

A HARD LIFE FOR BABIES

The life expectancy of a baby born even a century or two ago was very different from that of a baby born in 2015, no matter where in the world he or she lived. Doctors didn't yet understand the causes of disease, there were no antibiotics, and surgery was performed with unwashed hands and tools and without anesthetic.

The human life span is long enough today that some babies are lucky enough to meet their great-grandparents and even their great-great-grandparents. MUELLEK JOSEF/ SHUTTERSTOCK.COM

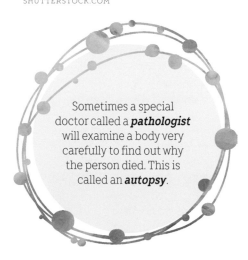

Sometimes a special doctor called a *pathologist* will examine a body very carefully to find out why the person died. This is called an *autopsy*.

If you take a walk in a very old cemetery, you might see the graves of many children. In 12 years the Hayward family lost five children between ages 11 months and 17 years.
MERRIE-ELLEN WILCOX

Sometimes babies die before they are born. This is called **miscarriage** when it happens in the first months of the mother's pregnancy. If it happens around the time the baby should be born, it is called **stillbirth**. It may happen because of a physical problem or illness in either the baby or the mother, but often the cause isn't known. And even though no one yet knew the baby, his or her death can feel like a huge loss for the parents and other family members.

Many babies didn't survive birth or infancy, and at least a third of children died before their ninth birthday. During the Middle Ages, parents in Europe dressed their young children like adults to trick death into looking elsewhere for its prey. Those who did survive childhood then had to face diseases that affected everyone, not just children, such as smallpox, dysentery, tuberculosis, cholera, typhoid and plague.

Women gave birth to many more children than they do in North America and Europe today, because they knew that a lot of them would probably die. Sadly, women still have to do this in many parts of the world where poverty, lack of clean water for drinking and no access to medical care often cause babies and young children to die.

GIMME SHELTER— AND FOOD AND WATER

Like all living things, humans have certain basic needs, starting with food, water and shelter from the elements. If these basic needs aren't met, we can't survive.

How long someone can go without any food at all depends on things like that person's size and how healthy he or she is. The Indian leader and activist Mahatma Gandhi fasted (went without food) for twenty-one days when he was in his seventies. Some scientists say humans can last for thirty to forty days without food, while others think we can survive for up to fifty-six days (eight weeks), as long as we have plenty of water. Chronic hunger, when people don't have enough food for a long time, will damage and weaken the body, making it more likely to succumb to illness and disease.

We can last for a much shorter time—only two to three days—without water, since we need eight to ten cups of water to replace what we lose each day. Without clean water our kidneys are unable to function, which affects the rest of our body.

Humans also can't survive outside a fairly small range of temperatures. Clothing and shelter help, of course, but we can't handle exposure to extreme temperatures. For example, people who fall through ice into water will typically die within twenty to thirty minutes if they aren't rescued. Their body temperature drops, body processes like breathing slow down, and their heart slows and loses its rhythm before finally stopping.

At the opposite extreme, being very active in temperatures above thirty-five degrees Celsius (ninety-four degrees Fahrenheit) when the air is humid (full of moisture) can cause body temperature to rise, damaging the body's systems and eventually causing death. Being exposed to high temperatures in very dry air for a long time can cause the body to lose too much water and salt, also leading to death.

For centuries people have tried to find ways to live longer. Today a small number of people are having their bodies preserved through **cryonic suspension**, in the belief that someday medical science will be able to cure them and bring them back to life. The body is frozen right after death and then stored in liquid nitrogen at very low temperatures (–196 degrees Celsius, or –320 degrees Fahrenheit).

PHOTO COURTESY OF ALCOR LIFE EXTENSION FOUNDATION, WWW.ALCOR.ORG

THE ROPE TO HEAVEN

In East Africa, the Nuer people tell of a time long ago when heaven and earth were tied together by a rope, and there was no death. People lived forever, because when they got old they could just climb the rope to heaven and be made young again before returning to earth.

Animals weren't allowed to climb the rope, but one day a hyena and a weaverbird did. The High God said they were not allowed to return to earth, where they would certainly make trouble. But one night they escaped and climbed down the rope. When they got close to the ground, the hyena cut the rope, and the top part of it was pulled up. From that day on, people grew old and died because they had no way to climb to heaven. SAVEJUNGLE/SHUTTERSTOCK.COM

LIMBO

Do you believe in ghosts? Many people do. Usually a ghost is believed to be the spirit of a dead person who hasn't made it to the afterlife and is stuck in our world in a kind of limbo. "Good" ghosts aren't considered harmful—they just hang around, sometimes making their presence known by appearing or making noises. "Evil" or "angry" ghosts often have unfinished business, maybe because they were treated badly in life, or they died violently, or they were just plain nasty. These are sometimes called demons. Many cultures have people who say they know how to make ghosts move on to the afterlife and leave the living in peace.

In fact, ghosts are just one of many types of **undead** beings, or living dead, that can be found in myths and legends from around the world. The undead are dead people who behave as though they are still alive. Some, like ghosts, don't have a body. But others, like **zombies** and **vampires**, have a body and use it to harm the living.

The idea of the zombie came from Haiti, where people believed that witchcraft could bring a corpse back to life. Zombies and the zombie apocalypse, where living people are turned into zombies, are popular in horror and science-fiction novels and movies.

Vampires, undead beings who feed on living humans, also star in scary novels and movies such as *Dracula*. They were very common in the folklore of Eastern Europe, although similar creatures can be found in the stories of many cultures throughout history. All of these cultures had special ways to protect the living, such as eating garlic or smearing it on windows and doors. They also had methods for either preventing dead bodies from becoming vampires or destroying those that had become vampires, like pinning them to the ground with metal spikes.

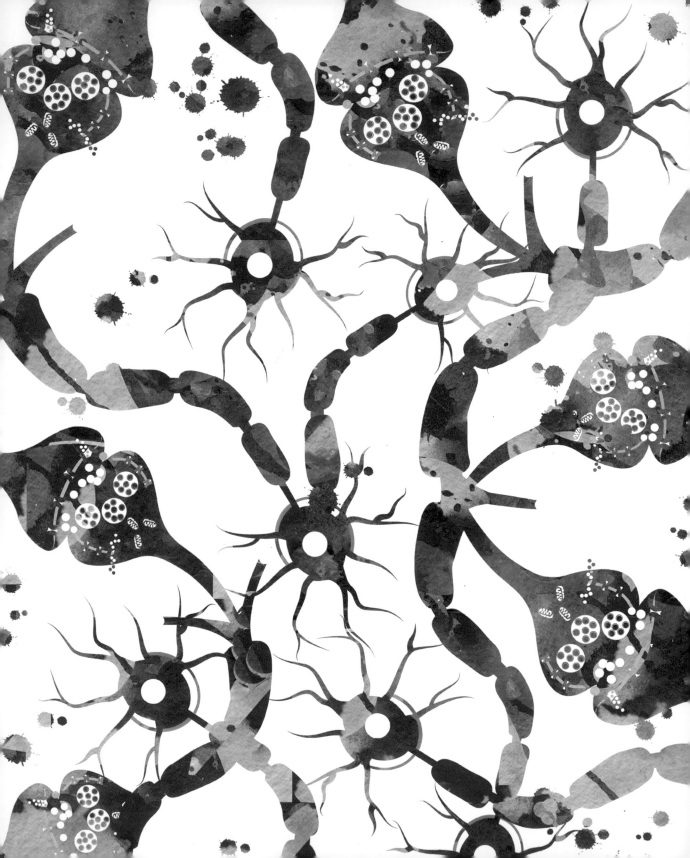

CHAPTER THREE

Nature or Science?

T hose of us who are lucky enough to live in countries like Canada and the United States have lots to thank modern medicine for. Most women survive childbirth, children usually survive childhood, and many of us live longer than we might have in an earlier time in history. But with all the miracles have also come some dilemmas that we've never had to deal with before.

Until the middle of the twentieth century most people died at home, surrounded by their family. Illnesses like polio, influenza, pneumonia and cholera killed babies, children and adults quickly. People with chronic diseases like heart disease and cancer couldn't be kept alive. Nature, not science, controlled how and when people died.

By the 1950s, though, new technologies and medicines were being developed that would allow doctors to prolong life by keeping bodies nourished, hearts beating and lungs breathing. Many lives could be saved that couldn't have been saved before. But this hasn't always been a good thing.

An early type of ventilator, known as an iron lung, helped people breathe when they were suffering from diseases like polio.
EVERETT HISTORICAL/SHUTTERSTOCK.COM

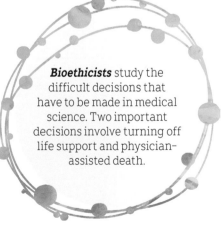

Bioethicists study the difficult decisions that have to be made in medical science. Two important decisions involve turning off life support and physician-assisted death.

29

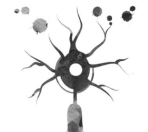

TURNING OFF THE MACHINES

Life support is what we call the medicines and machines that are used to keep people alive when they would not otherwise survive. The most common types of life support do the work of the lungs, heart, kidneys and digestive system. One of the best-known kinds of life support is the *ventilator*, a machine that pushes warm, moist and oxygen-rich air into the lungs. Another is the *feeding tube*, which provides a person with food and water when he or she is unable to eat or drink.

Being able to keep people alive for a long time with machines presents a dilemma. If a person is never going to recover, when should the machines be turned off? At the heart of that question lies another—when is a person still a person, and when is a person dead? Philosophers, religious leaders, scientists, doctors, politicians and the courts have had to deal with these questions. As a result, most places now have laws that say when and how life support can be turned off.

DRAWING THE LINE

Throughout history we have used different ways to identify the moment of death—when a person passes from living to no longer living. One of the most common was when the person had stopped breathing and his or her heart had stopped beating. An easy way to tell was to hold a mirror in front of the person's mouth to see if it got misty. If it didn't, the person was dead.

With today's medical technology, though, it has become harder to draw a line between life and death. Hearts can be

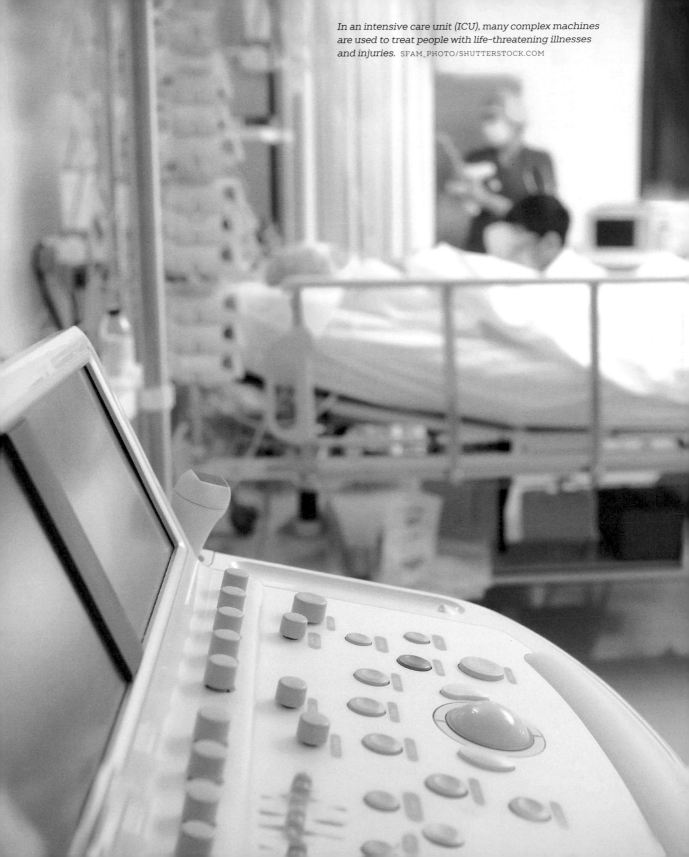

In an intensive care unit (ICU), many complex machines are used to treat people with life-threatening illnesses and injuries. SFAM_PHOTO/SHUTTERSTOCK.COM

As many as 50 people can benefit from the organs and tissues of one person who has died. STURTI/ISTOCK.COM

In a **will**, people tell others what they want done with their possessions after they die. Some people also have a **living will** (or **advance directive**), spelling out what medical treatments they want, or don't want, if they become very ill and can't communicate. A **do-not-resuscitate (DNR) order** tells medical staff not to use cardiopulmonary resuscitation (CPR) if a person's heart stops. These documents have been created because medical technology can keep people alive when they would otherwise not survive.

restarted and lungs kept breathing by machines, even when the brain has completely stopped functioning and the person cannot recover. Or a person may be in a deep coma with severe brain damage, but the parts of the brain that run the heart and lungs continue to work.

Today doctors often use the brain, rather than the heart and lungs, to confirm death. A person is dead when his or her brain is dead—when there is no electrical activity in the brain. In other words, **brain death** is considered to mean death.

PASSING LIFE ON

One of the most amazing advances in modern medicine is the ability to transplant organs and other parts of the body from one person to another. A person who has just died can donate as many as six organs, as well as tissues like skin, corneas (from the eyes) and heart valves, and as many as fifty other people can benefit. (Living people can also donate blood, a kidney and a portion of their liver or pancreas.) Knowing that a person who has died lives on in others whose lives have been saved or greatly improved can be very comforting for his or her family.

CARING FOR PEOPLE WHO ARE DYING

Doctors began to realize late in the twentieth century that a new kind of care was needed for people in hospitals who were *terminally ill* (not expected to recover). *Palliative care* helps people at the end of life with not just their physical needs but also their emotional, spiritual, cultural and social needs—and those of their families.

Palliative care can be provided anywhere—in a hospital or nursing home, at home or in a special place called a hospice, which is specifically for people who are dying. And palliative care is provided by a team of people that includes doctors, nurses, social workers, counselors, spiritual advisors and volunteers. The aim is to allow people to die with dignity and in comfort, and to help their families and friends cope with their loss.

HELPING PEOPLE DIE

Human beings have taken their own lives, or died by *suicide*, since the earliest days of recorded history. Suicide can be found in the myths and legends of the great civilizations.

CICELY SAUNDERS: FOUNDER OF THE MODERN HOSPICE

In a large London hospital after World War II, a social worker named Cicely Saunders became friends with a Polish refugee who was dying far from home. They talked a lot about the need to create more homelike places for people to die. When he died, Cicely decided to learn more about caring for people with terminal illnesses. She went back to school to study medicine, and after graduating she began to develop what would become palliative care. In 1967 she established the first modern hospice, St. Christopher's, in London.

DEREK BAYES/CICELY SAUNDERS INTERNATIONAL

Death doulas (also known as death midwives) help people who are dying, just as doulas and midwives help women giving birth. They work with both the dying person and the family to plan what they want to have happen both before and after death.

OSCAR'S SPECIAL POWERS

At a nursing home in Rhode Island, Oscar the cat spends most of his time doing his usual cat thing. But when Oscar was quite young, the doctors noticed that Oscar always seemed to know when a patient was going to die. A couple of hours before the death he would jump up on the bed to cuddle with the patient. He was so accurate that when he went to a patient, staff would phone family members and tell them to come to the nursing home. One of the doctors wrote about this in a medical journal, and Oscar the hospice cat became famous.

COURTESY OF DR. DAVID DOSA

Some cultures and religions accepted and even encouraged it, while others have been against it. For example, suicide was a crime in Canada until 1972, and it is still against the law in some countries.

There is also a long history of people helping others die. The original version of the Hippocratic oath, a set of rules that all doctors had to follow, was written in Greek in the fifth century BCE (Before the Common Era) and included the words *Neither will I administer a poison to anybody when asked to do so, nor will I suggest such a course.* This implies that doctors had been giving people poison when they asked for it to end their suffering.

Late in the twentieth century, people with terminal illnesses began to ask for the legal right to end their suffering themselves, with help from a doctor. Some countries, like

Switzerland, the Netherlands, Belgium, Luxembourg and most recently Canada, as well as Oregon, Washington and Vermont in the United States, have passed laws allowing *physician-assisted death*. This is only for people who are terminally ill and will never recover, and who are suffering from a lot of pain and other physical problems. They must also be able to make decisions and communicate their wishes.

Physician-assisted death is controversial, even in the places where it is legal. Religious leaders, philosophers, bioethicists, doctors and many others have strong opinions about it, and the debates will likely continue for a long time.

Physician-assisted death isn't the same as *euthanasia*, which means ending a life to relieve suffering without the person's consent. Sometimes we have to do this with our pets, but it is not allowed with humans in Canada or the United States.

PANDORA'S BOX

In Greek mythology, the Titans were a gigantic race who lived on earth before humans. The Titan brothers Prometheus and Epimetheus were given the task of creating man. When Prometheus stole fire from the heavens and gave it to man, the great god Zeus was angry and wanted revenge. He asked the god Hephaistos to make the first woman—out of clay. The goddess Athena brought her to life, the goddess Aphrodite made her beautiful, and the trickster god Hermes taught her to deceive. They named her Pandora ("all-gifts"). Then they gave her to Epimetheus, who had been warned by Prometheus never to accept any gifts from the gods. Epimetheus accepted Pandora anyway.

In his house, Epimetheus had a box (or a jar) in which he kept a bunch of nasty things that weren't used when he and Prometheus were creating man. Pandora was so curious about the contents of the box that she lifted the lid, letting all those nasty things escape. Envy, evil, illness and death would plague humans forever. The only thing left in the box was hope.

CHARLES-AMABLE LENOIR/WIKICOMMONS

BIRDS

Since birds can fly, they see and find out things that we usually can't. This might be why so many cultures have connected birds with death.

Sometimes birds are seen as **omens** of death. Have you ever heard that a bird trapped inside a house means someone in the family is going to die? This is a common superstition, especially in English-speaking countries. In different places, swallows flying down a chimney, whippoorwills landing near a door and crows landing on a garden fence are taken to mean the same thing.

Black birds like crows and ravens, night birds like owls, and any birds behaving strangely, like roosters crowing in the middle of the night, are seen by different groups as bearers of bad news. In China, the owl's call is heard as *wa, wa*, which means "dig, dig"—a grave will be needed soon.

Birds are also sometimes seen as psychopomps, creatures who carry the souls of the dead to the afterlife. For example, many Indigenous Peoples in North America believe that owls carry souls away. Other people, both in North America and in Asia, give that job to vultures. The ancient Egyptians believed the soul could leave the dead body in the form of a hawk, and they built their tombs with shafts that the birds could fly in and out of.

Where people believe the afterlife takes place underwater rather than in the sky, diving birds like kingfishers often carry the spirits of the dead to the afterlife. Other seabirds, like storm petrels and gulls, have been seen in various cultures as the souls of dead sailors and fishermen, warning the living of bad weather.

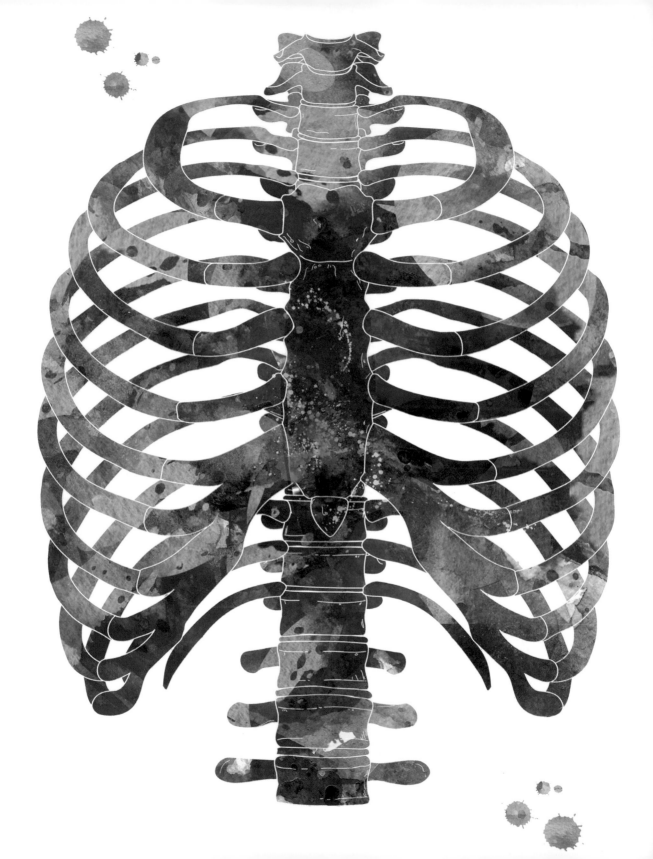

Atoms to Atoms

As you know from Chapter One, when a person dies, all the atoms used to build the molecules and cells in the body will eventually be used again in other living things. But in order to be recycled, the molecules and cells first have to be broken down. This happens through the process of **decomposition**.

Although you can't see much change in the body for the first couple of days (except in warmer temperatures, where the process is faster), decomposition begins about four minutes after death. The body cools gradually. Two or three hours after death the face and neck become stiff, followed by the rest of the body. This is called **rigor mortis**. It may last for up to three days, and then the body suddenly relaxes and softens again. Meanwhile, the bacteria and enzymes that did other jobs while the body was alive have begun to break down the body's tissues.

Left on its own, a body will take months and even years to decompose, and of course bones can last for millennia. Throughout human history, every culture has had ways of dealing with bodies before decomposition has progressed very far.

A stained-glass window shows a man on his deathbed—at home, surrounded by his family. Moments after he takes his last breath, his body will begin to decompose. JORISVO/
SHUTTERSTOCK.COM

What happens to a body after death?

MINUTES

In the first seconds after death, **BRAIN ACTIVITY** increases and then stops.

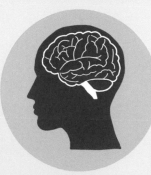

DECOMPOSITION begins about **4 minutes** after death, when cells deprived of oxygen begin to die.

HOURS

BODY TEMPERATURE drops by about 2 degrees Celsius (4 degrees Fahrenheit) in the **first hour** and by about half that each hour afterward, until it is the same as the air.

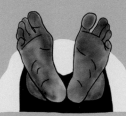

As soon as the blood stops circulating, it begins to settle in the lowest parts of the body, turning the skin in those areas purplish red. This is called *livor mortis*. It becomes visible around **2 hours** after death.

RIGOR MORTIS begins **2 or 3 hours** after death and lasts for up to 3 days.

MONTHS & YEARS

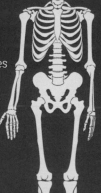

If a body is left at 10 degrees Celsius (50 degrees Fahrenheit), the soft tissues will be gone within about **4 months**, leaving just the SKELETON.

The process is faster in warmer temperatures, and slower in cooler temperatures.

Depending on conditions, the bones can last for as little as 10 years—or for thousands of years.

DAYS

As the skin dries out it begins to **SHRINK**, making it look as though the fingernails and hair are growing.

The tissues continue to break down, releasing chemicals that **SMELL** really bad.

WEEKS

The **BACTERIA** consuming the body are joined by insects. What we call maggots are the larvae of flies. They can consume the decomposing flesh within a matter of **weeks**.

About **2 days** after death, green blotches begin to appear, starting on the abdomen. This happens as the organs and other tissues are consumed by enzymes and bacteria, in a process called *putrefaction*.

But whether a body is buried, cremated, consumed by animals or tossed in the sea, the ancient atoms of which it was made will continue the cycle of life on earth.

BURIAL

Humans have been burying their dead for at least a hundred thousand years, all the way back to the Stone Age. *Burial* is a way to keep us from seeing the body as it decomposes. Sometimes it's used to keep diseases from spreading. In many cultures, burial is also a way to send the dead person on to the afterlife.

Many cultures throughout history have buried the dead in the ground, usually in a special place. In North America and Europe today, we often bury our dead in *cemeteries*. Many churches used to have their own cemeteries, which were known as graveyards. Each grave is marked, often with a gravestone—a polished stone with the person's name carved into it and the dates of his or her birth and death. Sometimes a gravestone contains the names and dates of entire families. Some people also have an *epitaph* carved on their gravestone—a few words that honor them or tell us something about them.

The dead may be placed in a *coffin* (or *casket*). As you can see on page 50, coffins may be very fancy or very simple. In some places the body is wrapped and buried in a cloth called a *shroud* instead. And different cultures bury their dead in different positions—lying down, face up or face down, curled up, arms crossed or straight. In some ancient cultures, warriors were buried standing up. Some societies even buried people upside down as a punishment. Muslims traditionally bury the dead with the face or the body facing the holy city of Mecca.

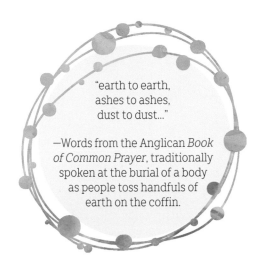

"earth to earth, ashes to ashes, dust to dust..."

—Words from the Anglican *Book of Common Prayer*, traditionally spoken at the burial of a body as people toss handfuls of earth on the coffin.

In the Jewish tradition, people leave a small stone or pebble when they visit a grave. The epitaphs on these gravestones in the Jewish cemetery near my home tell us a lot about the much-loved people buried here, and the stones show that their graves are visited often. (Bubie means "grandmother.")
MERRIE-ELLEN WILCOX

The Taj Mahal, in Agra, India, is perhaps the world's best-known mausoleum. The Mughal emperor Shah Jahan had it built in the 17th century to house the tomb of his wife, Mumtaz Mahal. DMITRY STRIZHAKOV/
SHUTTERSTOCK.COM

Sometimes the dead are placed in some kind of **tomb** or chamber instead of directly in the ground. There are many kinds of tombs. Some are underground. They might be as simple as a cave enclosed with rocks or as elaborate as a **catacomb**, a large underground cemetery consisting of large chambers and long passages lined with niches for the dead. Burial vaults and **crypts** were usually built under churches or churchyards. Other tombs, called **mausoleums**, are often built aboveground. They were originally built for important people, like the pyramids built for the pharaohs in Egypt, but today they can be built for anyone. (Sometimes they are underground as well.)

MUMMIFICATION

When you think of mummies, you probably think of the ancient Egyptians, Halloween or horror movies. Bodies buried in the hot, dry sand of the desert were preserved naturally, and the ancient Egyptians came to believe that preserving the body was an important step toward a person living well in the afterlife. They began to create elaborate tombs and perfected methods of preserving bodies. They did this by removing the organs and bodily fluids, leaving the body covered in salt for a period of time to dry it, rubbing perfumed oils on the dried body and then using thick layers of plant resin to glue strips of linen and a linen shroud around it.

But did you know that it wasn't just the Egyptians who made mummies? The ancient peoples of Chile and Peru, for example, used *mummification* as early as 6000 BCE, at least two thousand years before the Egyptians. Many other ancient cultures made mummies too, including those in Spain, Nigeria, Ethiopia, China and Tibet, as well as the Aztecs and Mayans.

The ancient Egyptians mummified their pharaohs (below) and other wealthy people who could afford to pay to have their bodies preserved. But they also mummified all kinds of animals, like this cat (above). Some were pets who were buried with their owners. Others were intended as food offerings for humans in the afterlife, and still others were sacred offerings to the gods. ANDREA IZZOTTI AND MIKHAIL ZAHRANICHNY/SHUTTERSTOCK.COM

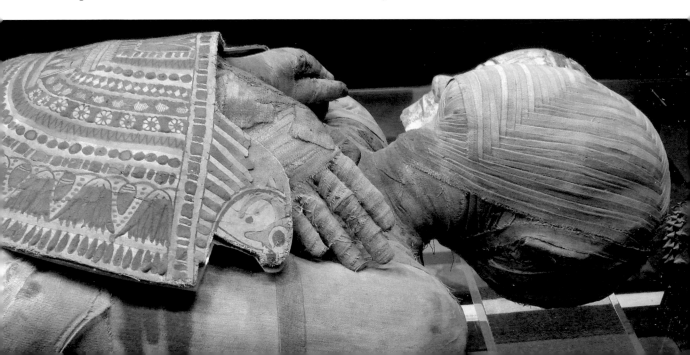

Hundreds of "bog bodies" have been found in northern European peat bogs like this one. KUTTELVASEROVA STUCHELOVA/SHUTTERSTOCK.COM

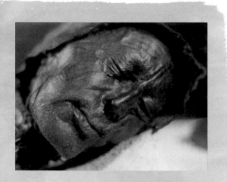

TOLLUND MAN

Tollund Man was discovered in a peat bog in Denmark in 1950. The mummy was so well preserved that the police thought he was a recent murder victim. But scientists found that he had died more than 2,200 years earlier. The acid in the peat, the lack of oxygen and the cool temperatures had preserved not just the body but the stubble on his chin, his hair and the animal-skin hat on his head. Even his organs were preserved, as well as his last meal. (In case you're wondering, it was a porridge of grains and seeds!)
WIKIPEDIA

Other conditions besides hot sand can preserve a body naturally. For example, the cool, damp conditions of peat bogs in northern Europe have created mummies (known as bog people), as have glaciers. When these natural mummies are found, researchers use science to determine when they died, and then they can learn a lot about how people lived in that time and place.

EMBALMING

The methods that ancient cultures used to make mummies were actually a form of *embalming*, or preserving human remains by treating them with various substances. In modern cultures, embalming is used to slow the process of decomposition so the body looks nice for funerals, for being transported to other places or for use in science. Modern embalming methods involve replacing the body's fluids with various chemicals.

Famous people, like political leaders (including Abraham Lincoln), popes, scientists and celebrities, have often been embalmed in order to preserve them for a short time or even forever. For example, Vladimir Lenin, the Russian communist revolutionary, was embalmed and has been displayed in a mausoleum in Moscow since shortly after his death in 1924.

CREMATION

Cremation, the burning of the body until its soft parts are destroyed by fire, has been practiced by humans for at least twenty thousand years. Although many cultures have

used cremation in different periods of human history, it was most established in India, where it became the preferred funeral rite for both Hindus and Buddhists.

Cremation was also common among the ancient Greeks and Romans. But the early Christians preferred to bury the dead, and cremation was forbidden by law for centuries in Europe, used only as an emergency measure during outbreaks of plague and sometimes on the battlefield. Cremation was reintroduced in Europe in the nineteenth century as a way to prevent the spread of disease and use less space for the dead than burial, as the population was growing rapidly.

Today about half of Americans and more than two-thirds of Canadians prefer cremation to burial. Cremation is done

Hindus believe that the souls of people who are cremated beside the Ganges River and have their ashes scattered in the water are released from the cycle of birth and death. People come to the city of Varanasi, one of the world's oldest cities, from all over India to pray, cremate their dead and even die. The funeral **pyres** *burn 24 hours a day, every day of the year.*
PAKSONGPOB KASEMPISAISIN/SHUTTERSTOCK.COM

Children watch vultures doing their work at a Tibetan Buddhist sky-burial site in Sichuan, China. JAN REURINK

Some North American Indigenous Peoples placed their dead in high trees or wooden structures, wrapped in robes or enclosed in a coffin of some kind, to keep them safe from the vultures and other wildlife. Once the body had decomposed, it would be brought down from the tree and buried in the ground.

at a *crematorium*, where a special furnace called a crematory is used to burn the body. The remaining bones are ground up and put in an urn or other container. Some people then bury the remains (sometimes called *cremains*), store them in a *columbarium* (a memorial building) or scatter them in a place that was special to the person who died. But there are some other, more creative, things people can do these days, like turning the remains into fireworks, artificial diamonds, vinyl records and even underwater reefs.

SKY BURIAL

In some parts of the world, where there is little soil in which to bury bodies and not enough wood to burn them with, people have relied on animals, especially vultures, to consume them. This is called *sky burial*, and it was used mostly by the people of Tibet, Mongolia, parts of China and other countries in the Himalayan mountains.

The Buddhists who live in these regions believe the dead body is simply an empty vessel, and there is no need to preserve it. They also believe that giving the body to the birds is an act of great generosity and compassion, qualities that are very important in Buddhism.

Sky burials are still performed in some parts of Tibet. And in Mumbai, India, some Parsis still place their dead on a high platform, called a Tower of Silence, for the vultures. They practice Zoroastrianism, an ancient religion that originated in Iran, in which fire, land and water are considered sacred and must not be used for dead bodies.

A Tower of Silence in Yazd, Iran, once used by people of the Zoroastrian faith to dispose of their dead. JULIA MAUDLIN/CREATIVE COMMONS

BURIAL AT SEA

Some religions require that bodies be buried on land or cremated, but that was hard to do when people died at sea, whether on long expeditions for exploration, fishing or trade, or during wars. With no way to bury them in soil or to cremate them, the bodies were "buried" in the sea. The body might be sewn into a shroud of sailcloth or a flag, or put in a simple casket, before being lowered into the sea. Weights were usually attached to the shroud or put in the casket to make sure the body sank.

A sailor in the US Navy is buried at sea.
U.S. NAVY PHOTO BY PHOTOGRAPHER'S MATE AIRMAN ROB GASTON

Burial at sea still happens sometimes, although it is more often cremated remains rather than a body that goes into the water. And there are lots of rules about where and how this can be done. Many religions, as well as navies, have special ceremonies and rituals that are performed for burials at sea.

TAKING IT WITH YOU

Qin Shi Huang (259–210 BCE) was one of the most powerful and wealthy emperors in Chinese history. He wanted to keep his wealth in the afterlife, so as soon as he took power he ordered the building of an underground palace where he would be buried. It took about 700,000 workers 38 years to complete it. Qin was buried there—with a Terracotta Army consisting of more than 8,000 life-sized soldiers, 130 chariots and 650 horses, all made of clay, who would accompany him to the afterlife. There were also clay acrobats and musicians, as well as dogs, pigs, sheep and oxen, all sculpted in amazing detail. The thousands of life-sized figures had been buried in deep soil for centuries, until they were discovered in 1974 by farmers digging in their fields. HUMPHERY/
SHUTTERSTOCK.COM

GREEN BURIAL

With more of us living on the planet than ever before, some people are worried about the environmental impacts of burial and cremation. For example, the chemicals used in embalming can leach into the soil and water supplies. Cremation uses a lot of fuel, whether fossil fuels or wood, and produces a lot of air pollution. But we still have to deal with bodies somehow.

Green burial, now allowed in some parts of Europe and North America, means burying a body without embalming in a simple shroud or container made from a natural fiber or sustainable wood. In Sweden there is a new method called promession, where the body is freeze-dried and crushed. Metals (like tooth fillings) are separated out and recycled. Another new process, called resomation, uses a chemical and heat to dissolve all the soft parts of the body, leaving only the large bones, which are then ground into powder and given to the family.

In Italy, Anna Citelli and Raoul Bretzel have designed an egg-shaped urn for cremated remains and a larger pod for a body. Made of natural materials, the Capsula Mundi urns and pods will be buried, like seeds, with a tree planted above each one, growing forests rather than cemeteries. FRANCESCO D'ANGELO/ CAPSULA MUNDI

WOLF AND COYOTE

In the history of the North American Shoshone people, Wolf is the creator. In ancient times, Wolf also had the power to bring the dead back to life by shooting an arrow into the ground under them. Coyote, the trickster, was jealous of the people's respect for Wolf and decided to trick him in order to turn the people against him.

Coyote told Wolf that he shouldn't bring the dead back to life, because soon there would be no more room on the earth for everyone. Wolf agreed, but he knew what Coyote was up to and secretly arranged for Coyote's son to be the first to die, as a punishment for Coyote's mischief. When Coyote came to Wolf and begged him to bring his son back to life, Wolf refused, reminding Coyote of his words.

This is how death and sorrow came to the Shoshone lands. Wolf is still respected; Coyote, not so much. SILVIE MIŠKOVÁ

COFFINS

People have placed their dead in coffins for thousands of years. Coffins have been made in all shapes and sizes and from all kinds of materials—clay, stone, lead, iron, wood, wicker and even cardboard.

The ancient Egyptians placed mummies of important people in mummy-shaped wooden or papier-mâché coffins and then placed those in large stone coffins, called *sarcophagi*, which were decorated with symbols telling the story of the dead person. The Greeks and Romans, as well as the early Christians, also used sarcophagi for their wealthy or important dead.

North American Indigenous Peoples used many different things for coffins, like canoes, baskets and the upper and lower shells of a turtle. On the west coast of Canada the Haida and Tsimshian people placed the remains of important chiefs in special totem poles called *mortuary poles*. And in Australia the Yolngu people place the bones of their dead in logs that have been hollowed out by termites, painted with the clan's symbols and then stood upright.

In Ghana special carpenters make elaborate coffins, often called fantasy coffins, for important or wealthy people. Carved and painted to look like airplanes, pop bottles, shoes, fruits and animals, the coffins are seen only on the day of the burial. A cheaper option—for people in places like England, Canada and the United States—is cardboard coffins, which come in different colors and patterns. You can even get a coffin that looks like a box of chocolates, complete with a red ribbon!

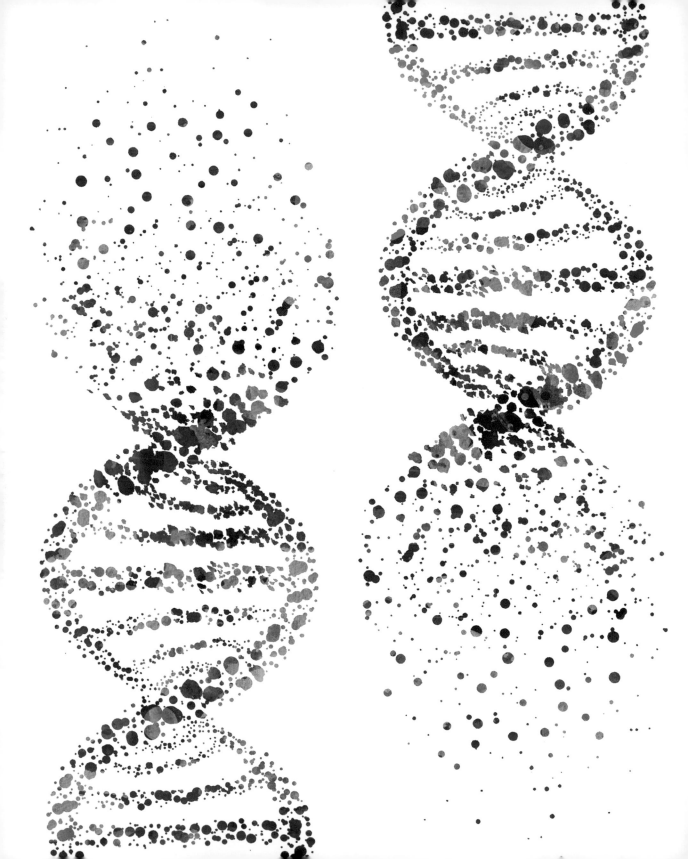

CHAPTER FIVE

Farewell, Adieu

In 19th-century England there were strict rules about how relatives of someone who had died could dress and behave. ISTOCK.COM/ILBUSCA

When someone dies, what we do with the person's body is only one part of the story. Humans and even some of our prehistoric ancestors have always performed special ceremonies and rituals after a death. There is usually a belief that how we handle the dead will affect not only what happens to the person in the afterlife but also what happens to the living. And once again, these *funeral rites* reflect our most important beliefs about life and death, so they are as varied and fascinating as we are.

WASHING AND DRESSING

In most cultures and religions, the rituals and ceremonies begin soon after the death with the bathing of the body, often by family members or friends. Different faiths have different rules for how the body is washed, and there may be special prayers that are recited during the process. In North America, bodies are often washed at the funeral home by someone who works there.

An **obituary** is a public announcement, usually in a special section of a newspaper, that a person has died. It normally includes a brief story of the person's life and information about a funeral or memorial. Some people write their own obituary before they die.

Once the body has been washed it is usually dressed— either in the person's best clothes or in special ceremonial clothes used only for burial. For example, in the Jewish tradition the body is dressed in simple garments made by hand from white linen or muslin. A man is also wrapped in his prayer shawl.

PRAYERS AND PARTIES

Many people believe the soul remains nearby from the time a person dies to when the body is buried or cremated. They consider it important to keep watch over the body during that time, often saying prayers or singing. In the Jewish tradition this practice is called *shemira*, from the Hebrew for "watching" or "guarding."

In the Celtic countries in Europe people also kept watch over their dead until they were buried, to keep evil spirits from harming the body. This was called a **wake**. Today, in many parts of the world, a wake is a kind of party held before or after a funeral as another way to honor a dead person. Wakes can sometimes be quite rowdy, with people making enough noise to "wake the dead"! The Greeks also had special games that they played only at funeral feasts.

Today we also have **vigils**, often at night, where people gather quietly, sometimes holding candles, to share their sadness about a death. People also leave candles, flowers, letters and other things outside the home of a person who has died or near the place where a person has died.

An Irish wake in the 19th century. Singing, pranks, games and stories were all part of the merrymaking, intended to help ease the suffering of the dead person's relatives. LIBRARY OF CONGRESS

A candlelight vigil in New York City to mourn the victims of the Sandy Hook Elementary School shooting. STACY WALSH ROSENSTOCK/ ALAMY STOCK PHOTO

PROCESSIONS

When the body is moved to where it will be buried or cremated, there is often a procession of mourners. In some places the procession is a time to display the status, wealth or achievements of the person who has died.

In some African cultures the body is removed from the home not through the door but through a hole in the wall, which is closed up right away to keep the dead from returning. The procession may follow a zigzag path, or thorns may be thrown along the way—again, to make it hard for the dead to return.

Here in North America the procession is often from the church or funeral home to the cemetery. The mourners are usually in cars, and they follow a special car called a *hearse* that carries the coffin.

Opposite: Women carry offerings during the cremation ceremony for a member of the Balinese royal family in Ubud, Bali. ALEXANDER MAZURKEVICH/ SHUTTERSTOCK.COM *Below: A funeral procession in Isalo, Madagascar.* DENNIS VAN DE WATER/SHUTTERSTOCK.COM

THE JAZZ FUNERAL

New Orleans is home to a unique procession called the jazz funeral. Traditionally, an important member of the community, often a musician and always an African-American, is "buried with music." A brass band consisting of horns and drums slowly leads the procession from the church or funeral home to the cemetery, playing sad, slow music. Once the coffin has been slid into place in the cemetery, the band switches to more upbeat tunes and accompanies the now dancing mourners to the next event. Strangers are welcome to follow the main procession in what is called the "second line." SHEILA/FLIKR

When an important public person dies—a prime minister, a president, a king or queen or an emperor—an entire country may have an official period of mourning. People might be expected to dress in the colors of mourning, government offices might be closed, and flags might be lowered or flown at half-mast (halfway up the pole).

When the much-loved king of Thailand died in October 2016, a year of mourning was declared. Many people wore black for the whole year, and more than 12 million people paid their respects as the body lay in state. At the end of the year, a five-day cremation ceremony was held. Here, thousands of black-clad mourners are gathered to grieve and sing mourning songs a few days after the king's death. 2P2PLAY/
SHUTTERSTOCK.COM

Members of a motorcycle gang in the Netherlands form a path for the hearse carrying the body of one of their members, who died in a crash. ROBERT HOETINK/ SHUTTERSTOCK.COM

In Victorian England, children were given "death kits" so they could practice mourning with their dolls. The kits included mourning clothes and coffins.

CEREMONIES

A *funeral* is a ceremony that is performed when a body is buried or cremated. Funerals usually involve a gathering of people and the use of special rituals from their religion or cultural heritage. The rituals might include prayers or other words, music and customs, like tossing handfuls of earth on a coffin that has been lowered into the ground.

Funerals are often, but not always, conducted by a spiritual leader. They might take place beside the grave or the funeral pyre, in a church or other sacred place, or in a funeral home. Sometimes family members or friends take turns speaking about the person who has died. This is called delivering a *eulogy*.

Today many people choose to have a *memorial service* instead of a funeral for a person who has died. This is a ceremony that happens sometime after a person has been buried or cremated. It can be held anywhere—in a sacred place, at a home or in a park or other special place outdoors. Sometimes the family decides what will happen in the memorial service. Sometimes the person who has died actually planned the service, telling the family where it should happen, who should speak, which songs should be sung or which music should be played. The person might even ask for a big party where people can have fun. Others ask to have no funeral or memorial service at all.

After a funeral or memorial service there is often a reception or even a banquet where people can eat and drink together in a more relaxed way. In many ancient cultures, including Greek and Roman, this would have been a large feast that could last for several days.

MOURNING

In some cultures the funeral marks the beginning of an official period of *mourning*. Every culture has its own set of customs for mourning. Often, relatives of the person who has died are expected to show their loss through the clothing they wear and their activities.

For example, Jewish people have a week-long mourning period called *shiva* (Hebrew for "seven"). Family members gather for seven days in the home of the person who has died and receive visitors. Traditionally they wear a piece of clothing or a ribbon that was torn at the funeral, a symbol of their grief. Candles are kept burning for the entire seven days,

BIG BUSINESS: THE FUNERAL INDUSTRY

Around 700,000 soldiers died during the American Civil War (1861 to 1865). Families in the North wanted the bodies of family members who had died in the fighting shipped home from the Southern battlefields. The only way this could be done was through embalming.

Embalming quickly became so popular that by the early 20th century it was simply expected. And since embalming couldn't be done at home by family members, a new industry was born—the funeral industry.

The undertaker delivered the body to a funeral home for embalming, washing and dressing. Funeral employees would make the body look good, often using makeup, before placing it in a fancy casket. Family and friends could then "visit" or "view" the body before the funeral ceremony, which often took place at the funeral home. The body could even be cremated there. The whole process could cost the family thousands of dollars.

Today the funeral industry earns billions of dollars every year. But it's also changing, as many people are looking for simpler, less expensive and more environmentally friendly ways to say goodbye.

In the Israeli film *The Seven Days*, a family sits shiva after one of their relatives has died.
PHOTO 12/ALAMY STOCK PHOTO

Queen Victoria during her long, long mourning, beside a portrait of Prince Albert.
ISTOCK.COM/WHITEMAY

and mirrors are covered so that, among other things, the mourners can focus on their loss rather than on themselves. People are considered to be in mourning until the thirtieth day after the death, the *shloshim* (Hebrew for "thirty")—or until a year after the death if the person who died was your parent.

In the past in Europe, people in mourning were expected to wear simple clothes, usually dark colored. **Widows** (women whose husbands had died) in particular wore special clothing, such as hats and veils. Even today widows in many European countries still wear plain black clothing for the rest of their lives.

Perhaps the most complex rules for mourning were in England in the nineteenth century. Women were expected to wear heavy black clothing, called "widow's weeds," for up to two years, then gray and pastel colors like mauve for another period of up to two years. Some women chose to wear mourning clothes for the rest of their lives.

Even the buttons and jewelry were made of jet, a type of coal, or fake jet. Men were also expected to wear black suits. And people in mourning were not allowed to go to social events. Queen Victoria, after the death of her husband, Prince Albert, in 1861, went into deep mourning, wearing black and rarely appearing in public for the remaining forty years of her life.

But no matter how a society expects people to show that they are mourning, or what rituals a culture or faith has for dealing with its dead, there is something we all share when someone close to us dies. It's called grief, and that's what we're going to look at in the last chapter.

My friend Hugh Davidson often wore a big orange scarf. At his memorial, many people wore orange scarves or hats in his honor, not knowing that others were going to do the same.
DAVID PROTHERO

ADAM AND EVE

In the Book of Genesis (the first book of the Christian Old Testament and the Hebrew Bible), God created the first man from the dust of the earth, and the first woman from the man's rib. Adam and Eve lived in the Garden of Eden, a paradise filled with beautiful trees, animals and birds. God told Adam that he could eat the fruits of any tree in the garden except for one—the tree of knowledge of good and evil. If he ate the fruit from that tree, he would die. One day a crafty serpent tricked Eve. He told her that if she and Adam ate the fruit from the tree, they wouldn't die but instead would become wise, knowing good and evil, like God. So Eve picked and ate the forbidden fruit and then gave some to Adam so that they would become wise.

But when God found out what they had done, he banished them from Eden, condemning them to a life of hardship, pain and eventually death: "You are dust, and to dust you shall return." And just to make sure they wouldn't return to the garden and eat fruit from the tree of life, allowing them to live forever, God put cherubim (unearthly beings who served him) and a flaming sword at the gates. Adam and Eve never returned. BENJAMIN WEST/NATIONAL GALLERY OF ART/AVALON FUND AND PATRONS' PERMANENT FUND

COLORS

If you have ever been to a funeral, you probably noticed that most people were wearing black clothes. In many parts of the world black is the color of mourning, maybe because we link black with mystery or with sadness. In Western culture this dates back to ancient Rome, where mourners wore dark-colored togas made of wool. In the early years of Christianity, monks also began to use black for mourning.

But black isn't the only color people wear when someone has died. Other colors—including red, purple, blue, brown and gray—are used by different cultures and faiths to show that people are mourning. And it is white that has been used most as the color of mourning around the world and throughout history. White is often a symbol of purity, goodness and innocence, and it is the traditional color of mourning in much of Asia. Even in Western culture, white was traditionally worn when a child, or someone who had not yet married, died. It was also used by European queens in mourning and is still used in some places in eastern Europe.

The use of color is especially important in China. White is the color of death there, because it is a symbol of the unknown and of purity, and a person's soul is believed to be pure again after death. A white cloth may be hung over the door of a home to show that someone has died. The dead person is dressed in his or her best clothes—usually white, black, brown or blue, but never red. Red is the color of happiness and good luck, and it is strictly forbidden at funerals. It's believed that a person buried in red clothes will become a ghost! In some parts of China, the body is traditionally covered with a light blue cloth before it is placed in the coffin, and the face is covered with a yellow one. At the wake or funeral, family members wear different colors of clothing, depending on their relationship to the person who died. The sons and daughters of the dead person may wear black, and grand-children wear blue.

Traditions are always changing though. Today in Canada and the United States, for example, people are sometimes asked to wear a particular color—maybe the dead person's favorite color—or to wear bright colors instead of dark ones.

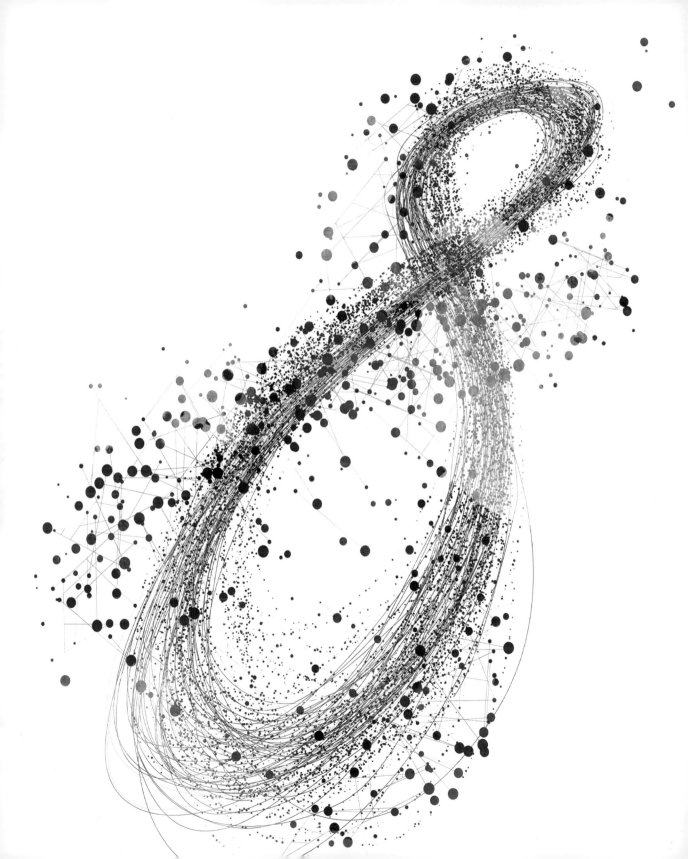

CHAPTER SIX

Healing After Loss

lot about death will always remain a great mystery. And as we've seen, our ways of dealing with that mystery are as varied as human beings are. But one thing is certain about death, and it's something we all have in common. When someone we know and love dies, we usually feel something called grief.

Grief is all the emotions, thoughts and feelings we have when we face a change like loss. We can have many emotions when we are grieving, but some common ones are sadness, fear and anger. We can also feel confused, lonely and stressed.

Grief is truly universal. Everyone, no matter where they live, what culture they are part of or what their faith is, experiences grief sometime, because we all experience loss at some point in our lives. But at the same time, grief is completely individual—every person grieves a little differently. There is no right or wrong way to grieve.

A family tending a grave on the Day of the Dead in Mexico. JAN SOCHOR/ALAMY STOCK PHOTO

Sadness is one of many feelings we might have when we are grieving. We all grieve when someone dies, but our grief is unique to each of us. ANNA JURKOVSKA/ADOBE STOCK

GRIEF IS A PROCESS

Grief is also more than emotions, thoughts and feelings. Grieving is a process we go through after we have experienced loss. The loss doesn't have to be related to death. We can experience loss when we move to a new town or country, when we change schools or when our parents divorce. Losing a friend, a sports championship or even a cherished thing can make us feel grief.

The process of adjusting to a loss is physical, mental, emotional, social and spiritual. This means that it affects our bodies, our minds, our feelings, our relationships with other people and our understanding of life. And, like any process, it takes time.

You might have heard of something called the five stages of grief. This was an idea developed by the psychiatrist Elisabeth Kübler-Ross in the 1960s. She believed that people who are dying from an illness like cancer go through five clear stages: denial (not believing they are dying), anger, bargaining (believing they can avoid dying if they change their ways), depression and acceptance. The five-stages idea was then used not just for people who were themselves dying, but for anyone who experienced a loss.

The problem with this idea is that people may think grief is a straight line, and that we simply move through each stage until we come out the other side and suddenly feel better. But, in fact, grief doesn't work that way. It's not a straight line. And the feelings don't come in any set order.

THE 8 OF GRIEF

A more helpful way to think about grief is as the shape of the number 8. We will each have different kinds of feelings on our 8 of grief, but the more positive feelings are on the top part and the darker feelings are on the bottom part. We move around and around our 8 as we move through our grief. On some days we might be on the top part, and other days on the bottom part, or we might bounce back and forth several times in one day.

Eventually we will spend more and more time on the top as we begin to heal from our loss. It might take a long time to get there. And we might suddenly find ourselves at the bottom again for a bit. But this is all normal.

THE 8 OF GRIEF

joy connection hope
understood forgiveness
optimistic sad
angry anxious
confused depressed
despair apathy
fear alone
isolated
suicidal

We will all have our own 8 of grief, so the feelings shown here might be quite different from yours. LEARNING THROUGH LOSS

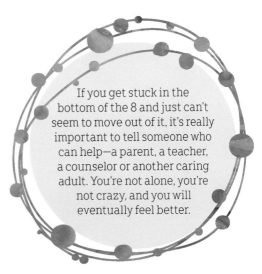

If you get stuck in the bottom of the 8 and just can't seem to move out of it, it's really important to tell someone who can help—a parent, a teacher, a counselor or another caring adult. You're not alone, you're not crazy, and you will eventually feel better.

Students learn about the 8 of grief in a school in Victoria, BC. Since we will all deal with loss at some point in our lives, it is important to learn about grief and how to help ourselves heal. LEARNING THROUGH LOSS

Bereavement is another word for the loss of a loved one. Grief or bereavement counseling is help for people who are grieving.

JUST GET OVER IT?

Nope. It doesn't work that way.

People often say this or some other version of it (be positive, look on the bright side, suck it up), especially to young people who are grieving. They might mean well, or they might simply have no experience of grief themselves, but it can be really hurtful and confusing if someone says this to you when you are in the turmoil of grief.

Grief can't be rushed—everyone has their own schedule. And it can't be ignored or buried. Grieving is a process we must go through in order to heal from loss. But it will get better.

TIME: THE GREAT HEALER?

Well, yes—and no. Grief is a process, and it does take time. How much time depends on the person. But it takes more than time to heal. We have to help ourselves heal.

If you injure yourself, you don't expect your injury to just heal on its own. If you have a cut, you'll probably clean it and maybe need to get stitches. If you sprain your ankle or break your arm, you might need a cast and maybe some physiotherapy later.

It's the same when you have had a loss. You need to participate in your healing. Be aware of your feelings and of where you are on your 8. Be patient with yourself. Do things that make you feel better, like being in nature, getting exercise or writing in a journal. And ask for help if you feel stuck at the bottom of your 8—or if you need help for any other reason, aside from grieving.

"Grief comes in one size. Extra Large. If we tuck it away in the bottom drawer where it never sees the light of day, it remains exactly the same. On the other hand, if we wear it, feel it, talk about it, and share it with others, it is likely that it will become faded, shrunk and worn, or will simply no longer fit."

—Raymond Moody Jr. and Dianne Arcangel, *Life after Loss: Conquering Grief and Finding Hope*

Support groups can be helpful for young people who are dealing with a loss or big change in their lives. The groups provide a safe space for sharing feelings, learning about grief and even having some fun. LEARNING THROUGH LOSS

Candles and flowers at a memorial for Amanda Todd, who died by suicide at age 15 after years of cyberbullying. Vigils were held in almost 40 cities around the world to remember Amanda and other victims of bullying.
JONATHAN HAYWARD/THE CANADIAN PRESS

WHEN SOMEONE DIES BY SUICIDE

If someone you know dies by suicide, you might have a lot of extra emotions, thoughts and feelings in addition to your grief. You might wonder why this happened, and if there was anything you could have done to prevent it. You might even worry that it was somehow your fault.

When people take their own lives, it's often because they had an illness in their mind that made their thoughts and feelings so tangled up and painful that they couldn't find another way to cope with them. It's a bit like when a healthy person dies suddenly from a heart attack—there was something happening inside the person that we couldn't see. And there was nothing we did to cause it and nothing we could have done to prevent it.

It's important to talk about your feelings and questions with an adult—a parent, teacher, counselor or someone else you trust—and probably not just once but several times, as your thoughts, questions and feelings change.

WHEN PETS DIE

Our pets give us so much love, and they are often an important part of our family. But dogs, cats and other pets don't live as long as we do. For many of us, the death of a pet is our first experience of a big loss. We are often surprised at how much grief we feel when a pet dies, whether from old age or illness or accident. People who haven't had a pet or who haven't had a pet die may not understand how it feels, but the grief we feel for a pet is just like our grief for other losses. It causes lots of different feelings, like sadness, anger and confusion; it's different for everyone. And it takes time to heal.

Because our culture doesn't have formal rituals for mourning our pets, it can be even harder to find comfort. We have to make our own rituals, like having a little funeral, burying the pet with his or her blanket or favorite toys, or marking the grave somehow. We can also make a scrapbook with photos of our pet, or a keepsake box containing mementos like the pet's collar, tags or toys.

A memory stone for Rehtaeh Parsons, who died by suicide after a sexual assault and months of bullying. After Rehtaeh's mother, Leah, started placing the stones in her daughter's favorite places, other people continued to put the painted stones in beautiful places around the world and send photos of them back to Leah. REHTAEH PARSONS SOCIETY

Our dog Alfa. When she died, we planted an oak tree near the spot where we buried her, and it has grown much faster than any of the others in our garden. We call it our Alfa Tree. MERRIE-ELLEN WILCOX

Campers at Camp Erin® Montreal, a bereavement camp, have the time to talk about their feelings. Talking or writing about your feelings or the person who has died can help when you are grieving. PETER FORD PHOTOGRAPHY/CAMP ERIN® MONTREAL

Making collages and other art can be helpful when you are grieving. At Camp Erin® Montreal, kids create a "memory board" to introduce the person in their family who has died. PETER FORD PHOTOGRAPHY/ CAMP ERIN® MONTREAL

WHEN YOU ARE GRIEVING

Here are some helpful things you can do when you are grieving:

- Take a walk and be in nature
- Get lots of exercise
- Get lots of rest
- Listen to music
- Dance
- Write in a journal
- Write a poem or story
- Write a letter to the person who died
- Read a book
- Draw or paint a picture
- Make a photo collage or a scrapbook
- Be with friends and family

WHEN SOMEONE ELSE IS GRIEVING

If we haven't yet experienced grief ourselves, we might feel uncomfortable being with someone else who is grieving a loss. We don't know what to say, so we just don't talk about it—or we even avoid the person altogether. That's a bit like saying "just get over it," and it can add to the person's sadness.

Here are some tips for being with someone who is grieving:

- First, don't avoid a person who is grieving, even if you don't know what to say. Staying away can make that person feel even worse.

- Tell the person that you care about them and that they are not alone. Keep being a friend. Ask what you can do for them.

- Don't be afraid to talk about the person who has died—unless the person who is grieving tells you he or she doesn't want to talk about it. Do say the name of the person and share your memories of them.

- Most important, listen. A grieving person may need to talk—a lot—about the person who died or about how the person died. That's part of the healing process.

We all need support when we are grieving. Remember to ask for it if you are grieving and to give it if someone you know is grieving.
ADOBE STOCK

THE EPIC OF GILGAMESH

The Epic of Gilgamesh is one of the oldest poems in human history. Written on stone tablets, it tells the story of the King of Uruk, who probably lived in Mesopotamia more than 4,500 years ago. When his beloved friend Enkidu dies, the king, or Gilgamesh, is driven by his grief and his fear of death on a journey to the underworld. He convinces the scorpion people to let him pass through a long, dark tunnel and is ferried across the waters of death.

On the other side he meets an ancient hero, Utnapishtim, and asks how he became immortal. Utnapishtim reminds Gilgamesh that only the gods determine life and death. However, Gilgamesh persists, and as a test Utnapishtim challenges him to stay awake for six days and seven nights. Gilgamesh is exhausted, and he immediately falls asleep. Utnapishtim's wife bakes a loaf of bread for each day that Gilgamesh remains asleep. When he awakes and sees the seven stale loaves, he realizes he is only human and that immortality is beyond his human powers. FRANCIS MOSLEY

FESTIVALS

Many people find it comforting to have special rituals for remembering someone who has died. This might be as simple as visiting a grave or another meaningful place, maybe on the anniversary of the person's death or on his or her birthday. But many cultures have festivals in which everyone remembers the dead on the same day.

In Mexico, for example, people honor the dead on November 2, the **Day of the Dead**. Especially in southern Mexico, people go to cemeteries, decorating the graves and leaving gifts of special foods and drinks, photos and toys, and candles and orange marigold flowers, sometimes called the Flower of the Dead. This is to encourage the souls of the dead to visit so they can hear the prayers and stories of the living. Sometimes blankets and pillows are left at the grave so the soul can rest after its long journey.

In Japan one of the biggest events of the year is **Obon**, a Buddhist festival when people honor their dead ancestors. The timing of Obon and the activities vary in different parts of the country, but it generally happens in the summertime. People visit graves and make offerings of food at altars in their homes or in temples. A special dance, called *obon odori*, is often performed. People traditionally put lanterns in front of their homes to guide their ancestors' spirits to this world, and at the end of the festival floating lanterns are put into rivers, lakes and the sea to guide them back to the afterworld.

People in China have a festival called **Qingming**, or Tomb-Sweeping Day, early in April. They visit the graves of their ancestors, leaving food and drinks and burning special sheets of paper called joss paper (or ghost money) to make sure that the dead have everything they need in the afterlife. There are also lots of springtime activities, like picnics and kite-flying, to celebrate the reawakening of nature with the coming of spring.

Conclusion

When I started to write this book, I was worried. Talking about death has been such a taboo in our culture for a long time. What would I find? Would it all be sad or scary? Would the research and writing make me depressed or anxious?

What happened was quite the opposite. Learning how we have dealt with death since the beginning of human history and in every corner of the world was like learning about what it is to be human. And once again I was amazed by how very diverse—and similar—we are. I'm so grateful to have had the opportunity to open the door to this fascinating topic, for myself and, I hope, for others.

Acknowledgments

So many people to thank for the miracle of publishing a book! I must begin, of course, with Orca Book Publishers—especially my wonderful editor and friend, Sarah Harvey, and designer Teresa Bubela, who so brilliantly brought the book to life. Thank you for letting the great adventure of *After Life* happen. I still can't believe how lucky I am.

Special thanks to Vicky and James Ballantyne for the week of undisturbed thinking, writing and gazing up the stormy Strait of Georgia in their island home. Your generosity continually amazes. Thank you, Yvonne Van Ruskenveld, for the private tour of Ross Bay Cemetery, and Congregation Emanu-El, Dr. Richard Kool and Howie Siegel for graciously allowing me to photograph the Jewish cemetery. A special bow to Louise Oborne (and her father), who introduced me to "the great mystery." Eve Joseph's book *In the Slender Margin: The Intimate Strangeness of Death* was and still is an inspiration.

Shauna Janz of Learning Through Loss (http://learningthroughloss.weebly.com) also inspired me—in so many ways. Thank you, Shauna, for the great work you do with youth and for supporting my own work on this book. The information you shared with me, based on the work of Learning Through Loss founder Sandra Elder, the presentations you allowed me to observe and your reading of the manuscript were all invaluable. I hope our paths will continue to cross for a long time to come.

Finally, to my family, thank you for your endless love and support. This book belongs to you.

Resources

There are many excellent picture books and novels for children that touch on the topics of death or grief—far too many to list here as resources. But there are very few, if any, nonfiction books for the middle-grade age group that address these topics. That's why I decided to write this book.

Listed below are the most important of the many sources I used for my own research and for the stories and histories from ancient and Indigenous cultures that appear in *After Life*.

PRINT

Béliveau, Richard, and Denis Gingras. *Death: The Scientific Facts to Help Us Understand It Better.* Richmond Hill, ON: Firefly Books, 2012.

Heinrich, Bernd. *Life Everlasting: The Animal Way of Death.* Boston, MA: Mariner Books, 2013.

Joseph, Eve. *In the Slender Margin: The Intimate Strangeness of Death and Dying.* Toronto: HarperCollins, 2014.

Kastenbaum, Robert, ed. *The Macmillan Encyclopedia of Death and Dying.* New York: Thomson, 2003.

Laqueur, Thomas A. *The Work of the Dead: A Cultural History of Mortal Remains.* Princeton, NJ: Princeton University Press, 2015.

Leeming, David. *The Oxford Companion to World Mythology.* New York: Oxford University Press, 2005.

Nuland, Sherwin B. *How We Die: Reflections on Life's Final Chapter.* New York: Alfred A. Knopf, 1994.

Ollhoff, Jim. *African Mythology (World of Mythology).* Edina, MN: ABDO, 2011.

Willis, Roy, ed. *World Mythology: The Illustrated Guide.* New York: Oxford University Press, 2006.

ONLINE

Encyclopedia Britannica, "Death Rite." www.britannica.com/topic/death-rite

First People of America and Canada—Turtle Island, "Wolf Tricks the Trickster: A Shoshone Legend." www.firstpeople.us/FP-Html-Legends/Wolf-Tricks-The-Trickster-Shoshone.html

History, "History of Death." www.history.co.uk/history-of-death

New World Encyclopedia, "Shoshone." www.newworldencyclopedia.org/entry/Shoshone#cite_note-7

World Health Organization, "Global Health Observatory Data—Life Expectancy." www.who.int/gho/mortality_burden_disease/life_tables/situation_trends_text/en/

Glossary

afterlife: the continuation of life after death

autopsy: an examination of a body by a pathologist to find out why the person died

bereavement: the loss of a loved one through death

bioethicist: a person who studies the difficult decisions that have to be made in medical science

Black Death: an outbreak of plague that killed as much as half of the population of the Middle East, North Africa, Europe and Asia in the fourteenth century

Book of the Dead: in ancient Egypt, a collection of spells that the soul needed to recite on its journey through the underworld

brain death: a state in which there is no electrical activity in the brain

burial: the act of placing a dead body in the ground

catacomb: an underground cemetery consisting of large chambers and long passages lined with niches for the dead

cell: the smallest unit of living matter, which works with other cells to perform the many functions of life

cemetery: a special place where people bury the dead; a cemetery at a church is known as a graveyard

coffin (or casket): a box in which a body is placed for burial

columbarium: a building where people place the cremated remains (or cremains) of the dead

corpse: a dead body

cremains: the ashes and bones that are left after a body has been cremated

cremation: the burning of a dead body

crematorium: a place with a special furnace (a crematory) for cremating bodies

cryonic suspension: the freezing of a dead body in the belief that medical science will someday bring it back to life

crypt: a chamber or vault for the dead, usually under a church or churchyard

Day of the Dead: November 2 in Mexico, when people honor the dead by visiting and decorating graves

decomposition: the process of breaking down all the molecules and cells in a body so the atoms they are made of can be used again

do-not-resuscitate (DNR) order: a document that tells medical staff not to try to keep a person alive if his or her heart stops

embalming: a method of preserving bodies by treating them with various substances

epitaph: words carved into a gravestone that say something about the person buried there

eulogy: a speech about a person who has died, given by family members or friends at a funeral

euthanasia: the ending of a life to relieve suffering *without* the person's consent or permission

feeding tube: a form of life support that provides a person with food and water when he or she is unable to eat or drink

funeral: a ceremony performed when a body is buried or cremated

funeral rites: the ceremonies and rituals that are performed after a death

green burial: burial without embalming, in a simple shroud or container made of sustainable materials

grief: the emotions, thoughts and feelings people have when they experience loss or some other major change

Hades: god of the underworld in Greek mythology

hearse: a car that carries a coffin

hospice: a place where people who are dying, and their families and friends, receive special care

immortality: the ability to live forever

industrialized countries: countries that have a complex economy based on lots of industry

karma: for Hindus and Buddhists, the idea that the way you live your life will affect your next life

life expectancy: the number of years people can expect to live, based on statistics

life span: the length of time that an organism can be expected to live

life support: the medicines and machines used to keep people alive when they would not otherwise survive

living will (or advance directive): a document that spells out what medical treatments a person wants or doesn't want if he or she becomes very ill and can't communicate

livor mortis: a purplish-red coloring of the skin in the lowest parts of a body soon after death

mausoleum: a tomb, usually built aboveground, sometimes for more than one body

memorial service: a ceremony that happens sometime after burial or cremation

miscarriage: the death of a baby in the early months of the mother's pregnancy

mortuary pole: a special totem pole that holds the remains of an important chief

mourning: a period during which relatives of a person who has died are expected to show their loss through the clothing they wear and their activities

mummification: the preservation of bodies by ancient cultures, using a variety of methods

nirvana: for Hindus and Buddhists, release from the cycle of death and rebirth to become one with the infinite spirit

obituary: a public announcement, often in a newspaper, that a person has died

Obon: a Buddhist festival in Japan when people honor their dead ancestors

omen: something that is believed to predict an event

palliative care: a special kind of medical care that helps people who are dying

pathologist: a doctor who specializes in identifying diseases and sometimes conducts autopsies

physician-assisted death: a person's legal right to end his or her life with help from a doctor

plague: a contagious disease that caused the Black Death

putrefaction: a process in which the proteins and tissues of the body are broken down, releasing foul-smelling gases

pyre: an outdoor fire for burning the dead, especially in India

Qingming: a spring festival in China when people visit the graves of their ancestors

reincarnation: the return of the spirit or soul to human life after death, over and over again

resurrection: the return of the dead to life

rigor mortis: a stiffening of the body that begins shortly after death and ends after two or three days

ritual: a ceremony that people perform, often to mark important events like birth, marriage and death

sarcophagus (plural is sarcophagi): a large stone coffin used by the ancient Egyptians and Greeks, as well as the early Christians, for wealthy or important people

shroud: a special cloth in which to wrap the dead for burial

sky burial: the use of animals or birds to dispose of bodies

soul: the spirit or energy that joins a body before it is born and leaves when the body dies; the part of us that many cultures believe to be immortal

stillbirth: the death of a baby close to the time when it is supposed to be born

suicide: the act of taking one's own life

terminal illness: an illness that cannot be cured and will cause a person to die

thanatology: the study of death and all the ways in which people today and throughout history think about and deal with it

tomb: a chamber in which the dead are placed

undead: dead people who behave as though they are still alive

undertaker: a person who prepares the dead for burial or cremation and often arranges and manages funerals

underworld: a place deep within the earth where souls go after death

vampire: an undead being that feeds on living humans

vegetative state: a state of unconsciousness caused by severe brain damage

ventilator: a machine that pushes air into the lungs of a person who would not otherwise be able to breathe

vigil: a gathering, often at night, where people share their sadness about a death

wake: traditionally a gathering to keep watch over a dead body until it was buried, but today often a party held before or after a funeral

widow: a woman whose husband has died; a widower is a man whose wife has died

will: a document in which people tell others what they want done with their assets and possessions after they die

zombie: a corpse brought back to life

Index

*Page numbers in **bold** indicate an image; there may also be text relating to the same topic on that page*